ALSO BY NATALIE SAFIR

POETRY

Moving into Seasons, 1981

To Face the Inscription, 1987

Made Visible, 1998

A Clear Burning, 2004

Love Like Snow, 2010

PROSE

Review: "The Poetry of Nursing" PoetsOn: 2006

"The Woman with Midnight Hair"
a Jungian fairytale 2010

"Ready Or Not" *Child of My Child*, Gelles-Coles, 2010

"Shashlik and More", Persimmon Tree, 2010

PRAISE FOR EARLIER WORK

from ***Made Visible:***
"I admire these utterly lucid, distilled, and powerful poems" –**Thomas Lux**

"Rarely does an author know and acknowledge the self as nakedly as Natalie Safir defines her inner life" –**Nina Cassian**

from ***A Clear Burning:***
"These sensual poems, at times ekphrastic or Jungian…or sacramental, resound in their 'fragile revelations'… a book of deep and wild sustenance."
–**Michael Waters**

"Musical, metaphorically daring, freshly seen and wise …Add to this a down-to-earth wit, and we have a poet whose work proclaims a sense of life lived, through a depth of grace that deserves our admiration." –**Colette Inez**

EYEWITNESS

poems
by

Natalie Safir

DOS MADRES

2016

DOS MADRES PRESS INC.

P.O.Box 294, Loveland, Ohio 45140

www.dosmadres.com   editor@dosmadres.com

Dos Madres is dedicated to the belief that the small press is essential
to the vitality of contemporary literature as a carrier of the new voice,
as well as the older, sometimes forgotten voices of the past. And in an
ever more virtual world, to the creation of fine books pleasing to the
eye and hand.

Dos Madres is named in honor of Vera Murphy and Libbie Hughes,
the "Dos Madres" whose contributions have made this press possible.

Dos Madres Press, Inc. is an Ohio Not For Profit Corporation and a
501 (c) (3) qualified public charity. Contributions are tax deductible.

Executive Editor: Robert J. Murphy

Illustration & Book Design: Elizabeth H. Murphy
www.illusionstudios.net

Typset in Adobe Garamond Pro & Dobkin
ISBN 978-1-939929-55-6
Library of Congress Control Number: 2016938828

First Edition

ACKNOWLEDGMENTS

The following poems have appeared in literary journals or e-zines:

The Westchester Review
    Old Witch
    Call it Romance
    Slipping Away
A Certain Slant of Light, Codhill Press Anthology
    A Meager Diet of Horizon
Ginosko Literary Review -
    Putting Lilli Down
    Woman, 1950 - deKooning
    Walking with Jesus
The Same
    Held Harmless
    A Larger Life
Hudson Valley Chronogram
    Roadtrip West
Slant
    Potatoes
Token, Univ. of Frostburg Press Anthology, G. La Femina, ed.
    My Line
Centrifugal Eye
    Rosa's Time (as Mary's Time)
Literary Currents - The River Reporter
    Gusts

To my daughters, grandsons, and loyal friends.

"And the point is to live everything. Live the questions now. Perhaps then, someday far in the future, you will gradually, without even noticing it, live your way into the answer."
– Rainer Maria Rilke, from *Letters to a Young Poet*

TABLE OF CONTENTS

AS IT IS

REVISIONS

AS IT WAS

AS IT IS

"Let's see the very thing and nothing else.
Let's see it with the hottest fire of sight."

Wallace Stevens from "Credences of Summer"

"The prologues are over. It is a question now
of belief... It is time to choose."

Wallace Stevens from "Asides on the Oboe"

Held Harmless

Former versions of myself
congregate on the bed --
some wring their hands,
shake and tremble, or
smile mysteriously,
while I have lost interest
in every one of them
except this current presence
touching fine cloth beneath her,
staring at leafed branches
overlaying the window,
absorbing green sensations
so that recollection, history
hold no currency.

Harmless stages
I cannot recover.

Why honor them
when each should have
known better,
and can change nothing?

Deflated, they creak
toward the door,
a ragged chronology
of scuff marks on the carpet.

Year End Meditation

This day carrying its burden of hope, freight of anxiety,
enlarges in my face like the eyes of the black boy
in a funny hat seeking my attention on the train.

Past holiday times have blown into a sky of years.
Where has it all been carried?
I am a pen that can retrace what's already written.

I anticipate every arriving bend of river, stone stationhouses
squat in their permanence, sky pale as a lover's hands
underwater, ducks sitting the currents.

This moment is a snow-heavy branch
thick with how long I have been observer and player.
A child screams out at the back of the train.

My daughter recounting her childhood loneliness
remains a cold howl on the back of my neck.
A grandson writes a letter about his happy day visiting,

saved along with postcards from my daughters' teen years.
Complaints, worries and achievements flood
my outline on the walls of their rooms.

The coal dark eyes of the boy, merry as I make faces
back at him, poke through my reverie, already gone
as the train lumbers into its next station.

I rise to continue a part of my story -- tall, bearded man
in a tweed coat eagerly waving as I step from every train
I have been departing and boarding for a quarter century.

Corridor

She walks down a long
corridor she has never walked before
between the tall surgeon who will
cut her body and the tall man
who promises to follow her to its end.

Walking behind she sees
herself watching them,
feet nowhere near the floor.

Thick burlap hangs between today and
a distorted image of a future
the doctors claim will be joyous
Oh, we will love and take care of you
as if you were our own --
if you follow our regimen,
do as we say, glory will be yours.

Her fingers grope the swaying curtain;
a hazardous solo course, to turn back
as sole caretaker of her condition --
one foot, the next, then the next,
the floor dropping further than
a reliable cure for her disease.

New Diction

Excision and re-excision, new words,
knife their way into my vocabulary;
hematoma loses its American Indian
resonance to lodge large and
purple above my ribcage -
a pound of flesh suddenly becomes
bloodied sheets visible
on the table of operations.

This is not about death, but
resistance to the regimen
of life saving procedures mapped
by the practitioners of health
claiming rights to my days,
months, thoughts and imaginings,
who control decisions in a larger system
that cripples my potency.

Who is the enemy here? The microscopic
cells that insist on multiplying
but belong to me?
An industry of experts on a disease
that defies understanding? The disease itself?
Why do they, who labor daily to save
lives assume diabolic procedures to
infuse killer chemicals and burning rays?

Let my body say what should be done.
Perhaps the force of physical destiny
demands to be obeyed, to claim dominion
over all of them who have pledged:
First do no harm.

Old Witch

The three- year-old looks up at me with puzzlement
and guarded fear and won't come too close.

It's the way my eyes are drinking in her being,
enjoying the contours of her little body, pert round

face. And suddenly, I feel in me myself at that age
frightened of a wizened grandmother who must have

held that voracious look as she delighted in
my presence, hungered for my newness with such

intensity-- I did not like it, did not want to be
around her. I called her a witch;   it was because

she wanted to eat me, that if I stayed pinned
to her eyes, she would lick me right off the bone.

Something Dark

Black squirrels are catching onto corners
of my eye; streaks of urgency,
comic triumph across leaf splattered lawns,
exclamation points traveling the wires,
their tails the final hook
of a question that shouldn't be asked.

Do black squirrels interjecting
markers across my path
reveal something dark, fleet
and inevitable I do not want to see?

Is golden light more splendid
framed by overhanging steely clouds,
does the wind sharpen its teeth
on our memories of summer ?

A Larger Life

The beech tree at path's end, a gray giant I called
elephant, has been dismembered by the ground crew.

Its blunt top took the brunt of the cuts, leaving
a thick column with a squared off high shelf

like an aircraft carrier waiting for war,
platform of vigilance and danger.

My tall friend stood with me at the ocean's edge
last summer as a choking black tide rolled in.

"There's no holding it back" she whispered to me
as if knowing within the year, ravaged by cancer,

her broad frame, scantily hung with flesh, eyes
draped with distance, would be cut down.

In my dreams, her ashes strewn across dark soil
generate rising stalks, new tough bark, blossoms

while from the brutalized stump of the elephant
tree, fragile green flags quiver in the wind.

Rosa's Time

Conference room,
room of night
where she moves toward the doctor,
one breast exposed.
Rooms without doorways,
shut-in rooms, locked
without exit or recourse.

Rooms without river bends,
jewels stippling a distant bridge,
skies brilliant with excitement,
white sails breathing green winds.

Hallways encounter thunder,
tangles of dark trunks,
a wilderness of pubic hair,
lovermen disguised as bears,
women without mouths
bearing stitch marks.

Her robe begins to unravel,
a twisty pile of chenille
on the office floor
where the doctor explains
his wordy theory to her body,
his plan of attack to the flesh,
neither looking nor listening
as the elevator takes her to surgery.

She gets off at the wrong floor,
though rehab is somewhere else
and it is after hours;
they will fashion her a new one,
an ice-cream dollop, cherry
and all on top and, like he said,
she'll feel nothing dragging
home her one-eyed body
without explanation.

Fears

A pinpoint of dark marks
where pain endings lurk,
the rest a sliver radiating
below as memory
swims its slim channel.

With a feathery stroke,
brush only the tip
and quick red daggers
remind you its substance
lies submerged.

Pick at it and
blood beads up;
dig and the tip recedes
into the shadowy fin
of last night's dream.

Soak it in warm
accepting oils
and what presents
you can recognize,
grab and pluck.

Even after you have
pulled it free
its phantom tail
slides up
and back below.

Alive by Night

Her long life lay
embedded in memory's batting
never to be unwrapped.

A forced amnesia by day --
her stake in the present towered
firm as the mast of a clipper ship.

By night, memory's webbed fingers
part the labia of outlawed dreams, travel
her locked womb to portals of the brain.

Archival scenes of sweaty bodies,
passionate encounters rooted in paradox,
a boy drowning in his own secretions.

No one has a face.
The screen of the dreamer
is engorged with emotion.

She is switched back to *what will not
stay dead* -- archeology of decades --
reckless detours, pointless sacrifice.

Pilloried by recognition, her eyelids snap open --
face flushes, moist pink sheets glossed
by an illuminating dawn of sanity.

It is 5 am, how will she survive
a senseless life, escape each unforgiven act,
all she had hoped to drown?

Morning is a mirror she must bury to its neck,
submerge a punctured hourglass,
its grit spilling away the sunshine.

I Do, I Do, Ramona

know how it is --

Fear trembles your spine
  when your legs begin to fail.

Your eyes fill with somber clouds
  when the family has left.

They are empty cups
  as you enter a room
then drop into slots
  between floorboards.

The delicate needle of your compass
  spins rootless
  in the mildew of memory.

  Is not remembering, perhaps a gift?

  *Am I pretending to know as I too
  move closer to the dark?*

Time

may solidify, frozen moments --

eyes lock together in a bottomless gaze;
blood streaks the urine bag
hanging next to her bed;
two towers flame in a blue sky

Evaporate into a steam of excitement --

a brush soaked in yellow
streams across a canvas
to the next swirl and the next;

glass mosaic shimmering
as light fires each piece;
his large hands enter her body

Or shatter in an explosive crash --

she flies out the cardoor onto the white line;
bullets zing through a window and find the child

Stagnate into a heavy puddle --

the tiresome lecturer refuses to conclude;
the line does not move toward the entrance

Distill into segments --

the sonata floats her over distant hills;
she drowns in a blue whirlpool of disremembering,
she knows but her fingers cannot reach

Back up to clog a drain or bubble
    into rapids at a terminal juncture

Time is running water rushing through our lives
Its river carries you, your cargo on its wide shoulders

    back to the adolescent studying herself in the mirror;
    forward into a desperate knowing

Rain everywhere soaking the body
Rain soothing levels of pain; rain falling and fallen

Immersion whether you flail your arms about
or feebly advance; it moves through you
as you/we move *(through it*

Slipping Away

Letting the cord drop from your hands,
the kite string you clutch sail up out of sight,
unlatching the cage that holds the crimson bird;

Praising the sun as it slides down a slot in the hill,
watching your shiny boat of dreams round
a faraway curve; waving adieu to the fires.

Allowing the sand, the years, the voices
to wash down your legs until only
echoes rebound from hollow rocks;

Releasing the starred night, an infant's smile,
the house that felt like home, that first
bite of melon, desire's electric dance;

Holding the urn of ashes where the cat used to lie,
the photograph that once was your mother,
a lover's voice on a tape you cannot find.

Reaching Forward

I phone my daughter in New York
to find out what will be
happening in three hours.

At the airport
my continuous present
travels with my luggage
into time coming
like an illness
I have already survived.

If I board another plane
swallow up
six more hours
I'll be caught up
on the bombings
before they happen.

Across the date line
tomorrow's hooded fairy
slides over the zenith
uncovering consequences
of today's decisions.

My daughter is a telescope
into a then I shall never live.

Will I be able to see
through her eyes?

Will we be able to signal
across the zones the way
my white-haired mother
turns up weeping bitterly
in a dream and I am
a nine year old reaching for her?

Old Woman Walking by the River

As wind kneebends the reeds,
the woman's back curves into distant hills;
her white hair flies in waves.

I join this woman who continues
expecting that the path will
carry her as it goes on.

It is not that I grew up expecting
nothing, trusting only
that the road cannot end here.

We push forward, parallel with
the wide river as tongues
of late afternoon whisper: **ever, ever**

The Woman Who Stands

When my children were little
we used to see *The Walker*
pacing Broadway from one end
of the village to the other,
a metal windup toy at her daily job.

A woman in our community
we labeled *The Woman Who Stands*
stuck in the tides of time
on winding paths in all weather.

In my village, a man wearing
a counterfeit Marine uniform
marches the streets, cell phone at ear
barking orders to his troops;
the Patroller checks each
street corner for unseen terrorists.

I joked about *The Walker*, the others
were objects of amusement.

These days indoors and out, unsure
of my intentions, shifting realities move
through me; I recognize bits
of myself in each of them.

There Seem to Be Oceans

The car was removed first; it had driven
itself up over the curb at the supermarket.

The favorite dog died suddenly without
explanation; a chubby white one
she really loved was given to an old friend.

She could still fumble with the tv remote,
chomp on candy bars and chips;
the programmed buttons on her cell phone
glowed unnoticed morning till night.

Keys and choices were disappearing.
The daughter regularly stuffed cash
in her wallet, kissed her and repinned
housekeys to her purse strap.

A day or year were illusive details;
names had spun into clouds of wonder.
Her grandson's smile
drifted away on a soggy wind.

Hair was lifting from her scalp.
The weather of her mind whirls above
precipitous blankness, while underground
a torque of terror restrains her.

Traces of blue watercolor float across
her narrowing band of life.
    She looks to the sky -- there seem to be oceans,
    a few colored birds seeking land.

Selective Amnesia,
Surcease and Release

Apoptosis: *in human embryonic development, certain cells are genetically coded to disappear at the proper time*

Magical, lethal blessing
that causes the death of interstitial memory,

untenable images coded to relinquish power and
influence, absorbed into faraway history --

Drops of my dying mother's blood
spreading into the urine bag when I should
have screamed for the nurses;

Annie's thud on the subway floor,
her eyes in the ward wild with desperation;

My brother trying years to mend his breaking
heart without the tools for restoration;

Images that would dissolve into ephemera
like the last eggs my ovaries shot off
when everything else was too late.

What lingers in me molders, failing
to conform to its genetic program,
while science develops a helmet
to select and destroy painful memories.

I dream of waking one morning
to such lightness I could grow spires,
float into azure, weightless.

Echocardiogram

Ecological earth strata fill the screen
with an ancient topography
the whoosh of arctic winds
plunks and clicks
locks of a canal
emphatic swahili syllables

an odd music of industry --
ash cans, tin drums,
the rhythmic jangle
of keys unlocking busy chambers
of the heart factory
doing its work

My heart shouts *'foul weather, foul weather'*
over and again, then whispers
'wooly forecast'
lowing lowing, holy holy

The probe is pointed beneath my ribs
to explore the soggy bottom of a heart
few have wanted to know

This old muscle, vessel of blood
and tears seems committed
to what it is doing
talking to me as it proceeds uphill
a gifted laborer bearing
the weight of its history
a heavy booted Ukrainian soldier
still expecting victory

Wandering Road

Pretend it's okay that the snow
coming down buries the bench
by the river where two dreamers
cling to watch years behind them
sketch a wandering road.

Pretend it's okay that each decade
ended farther from home and
their footsteps could not be corrected,
wiring tangled their tongues
delaying clear translation.

Pretend it's okay that the dreamers
have gone their separate ways,
their roads redrawn by too many storms.

Pretend this day is freshly risen,
and hearts are tender flexible muscles;
pretend.

The Mountain

The dream we hold is no more solid than the silvery presence
of Mt. Rainier, floating on a platform at horizon's edge --
a cone of petrified smoke, a pyramid of shimmery ash.
Its ancient geometry suggests a promise of permanence.

While we walk, or from the deck of a boat crossing, it reigns
as moon god of the east, crooning a soliloquy of compelling beauty.
Seen at a great height -- it is a whale freezing as it crashes
through water -- apparition of a life not lived.

Friend, its frosted façade prompts us to accept that
our desires dwell only in the realm of the unreachable.
How take our small goals seriously when flux
is the state of life's incomprehensible map?

Clouds

Without clouds, we would be tyrannized
by our one indomitable star;
left to gaze up at flat blue canvases
devoid of arcs to the imagination;
what would hold the rain within
strange irregular borders? Where
could its replenishing sheets be stored,
its drizzles of crinkly lace curtains
interrupting daylight's glare;
where else would blacks, deep charcoals and
cooling grays of late afternoon find legitimacy?
And the resplendent rolling whites containing
indigos, lilac and cerise folds at end of day?
Where could all our secrets hide, our
forgotten stories, and how would the winds
telegraph coming change?

Solstice

Snow ceased some years ago
when my world changed direction.

No fat satiny crows strutted on the sidelines
no squirrels streaking toward aerial hideouts
no blue air fragrant with moisture on the hills.

My rhapsodizing has fallen into disrepute;
I am recollecting snow the way I no
longer remember being young.

REVISIONS

Mind of Spring

after a poem by Wallace Stevens

You must have a mind of spring to regard
the boughs punctuated with green lace

and have been comfortable a long time
to behold the dazzle of forsythia

radiating in morning sun and not think
of sorrow hiding in the coming winds

that bring tattered petals down
to the course of their lives, the circle

toward sundown, when the onlooker
who watches the path as eyes and mind

studies the cycle of all circles and
feeling himself turning, is not afraid.

There Would Still Remain

after a poem by Wallace Stevens

Fresh cut daffodils in a clouded glass jar,
radiating yellows topping spring's return;
pale green legs lift their ruffled flags to the day.

What if we could anchor just one blossom
and make it whole,
a sanctuary in a sunny world?

Imagine this fine simplicity
erased all men's fears
and concealed the tormented I
reconfigured in a unified noun.

An inner world of placid water
fringed with rousing color
and permanence in the bloom.

Still, one would want more
need more, more than
the stability of color and form.

One would always need more --
futility is so deep in us
the sorrow so deep in us.

There would still remain the restless soul,
a need to escape courting
the meaning of it all, however simple.

This striving, lying in flawed perceptions,
tangled ideas and stubborn hungers
is our maddening hell.

When the Glad Words

When the glad words like pleasure, grand and amble crawled
    off to the armpit
of an old jacket and refused my calls, when the writing inside
    my eyes spelled only
gibberish and each day melted like rancid butter into stale
    bread, I asked
the woodpecker what he thought he was doing on the tree,
    asked the squirrel
about his busyness; inquired of the crow why he labored with
    that twig to whittle
it into a tool. And why their enthusiasm for such thankless jobs.

Nowhere is a hollow word; when the ground beneath tilted
    at a precarious angle
I was in the middle of scrubbing the keyboard so the letters
    would know who they were
and might be used to scribble a plan indigenous to me
    but the glad words
lacking arms turned grim like *insipid, worthless, rue.*

Woman, 1950

from a painting by W. deKooning

If I were a botched autopsy
sitting on life's toilet bowl
hands and feet amputated
breasts unevenly weighted
by clotted nipples
hair a stain of orange seaweed,

I could be that Woman.

Tattered body blown apart;
the geometry of my pubis
was bisected in a different era.

Two big eyes dominate my face.
I carry the simple helplessness
of a doll crying *Mama;*
she cannot resolve her missing belly
or utter long words from a sketchy mouth.

I am a preposition to grotesque form
even the artist cannot reconcile.

Is This Hope?

from the painting Hope 1, 1903, by Gustave Klimt

Hope supports a large stretched belly,
the fleshy baby curled inside unable to move.

Her ashen face stares
audaciously at her viewer.
Eyes carry fearsome wonder.

Burrowing into a carotene nest of curls
that stars float across,
a lowered jaw gnaws at her head

and from the immanent blackness behind,
the half lidded eyes
of a gaunt widow beam rage.

Hope rests her slender hands
on a perfect oval belly
protruding into the black,
legs posed before a rapture of fabric.

She knows the child pushing
to be born is the seed of her sorrow,

that her anguish will cure nothing.

L'Arlesienne

after a painting by Vincent Van Gogh

Seated at this table,
vivid daydreams arrive
like waterfalls in a desert
and I have no choice
but to muse on love.

I have been captured
by the folio before me,
its tattered blue pages a water ride
in a dory we rowed into twilight,
the gyre of your rugged forearms
promising me pleasure.

These tattered pages
hold fragile letters
stuffed between the leaves,
my open handwriting
leaping excitedly across borders,
my ardent script frightened
of its message.

Ah love, how I draped
your scarlet around me
more fervently than a flag,
how your wide stance
framed every threshold
forcing out forest wolves
gathering I would not hear.

Boats of Ste. Marie

from a painting by Vincent Van Gogh

The moored trawlers resemble awkward,
bent boots left behind on a pebbly shore.
Twiglike masts stretch toward
sister ships out in the channel.
Their folded sails implore the wind
to dispatch them to bluegem seas.

Taut lines angle to the wind's howl.
Weathered wood creaks from each carcass
moaning for the vast opening.
Beached, they remain breath's exhaustion,
whatever holds us back from adventure.

Harbor Scene

from a painting by Paul Klee

The crescent blue sloop of water is crossing,
its needle mast threads a watery sky upward into the ether.

Behind, inkline steps climb to vaporous buildings,
a hilltown where single strokes hide the depth of a vacant church.

The sloop will not drift out of the present into confrontation
with the geometry of responsibility and loss.

It rests in the exact space it belongs, boat of water
floating in two dimensions of simple dreams.

The Swan

I had only to step out
on the house's deck, lift my hand
and sliding forward he seemed
a cargo ship coming home.

His raised wings a cage of tulip petals,
arced above the stalk of neck;
he came across the pond
as a soundless glide of light
black feet slapping on shore.

What power Leda must have felt
"her thighs caressed by the dark webs"*
as his ardor broke over her,
knowing his understanding met her there.

*W.B. YEATS – "Leda and the Swan"

Scarlet Macaw

Straw thatched plain-faced man
slouching on the weathered bench
at the bay beach
waits to be asked by passersby
about the large bird atop his shoulder
as Paco, the scarlet macaw, sits erect
on his grey sweatshirt,
a striking epaulet one foot tall

Paco feels the urge to begin his walk,
descends the bench as staircase,
wobbles toward the sea
stopping at the tide line,
and up and back along it
carefully searches for morsels,
a hesitant old beachcomber
with splendor of leaping plumes
fires of blue and red shouting
across the drab sand

Don't you fear he'll fly off? they ask
-- no, he has been indoors
too long, those muscles are gone,
I recount to my 90 year old friend
confined to her apartment

and watch the red image
swirl toward her
rising on technicolor wings
from her chair to the outdoors --
flag of her spirit
waving above a trapped body
scarlet insignia above beige walls

AS IT WAS

'By now I too have become a storage tower of memory'
Lisel Mueller from "Pillar of Salt"

"I wanted to stay in September"
Nina Cassian from *Life Sentence*

End of War Alerts

Mother covered her raven hair with a white linen cloud
intoning Sabbath prayers before the candles;
her good nature and the solid aroma of Sunday's
potroast reawakened our appetites;

frequent visits of worldly aunts for mah jong
or four- handed bridge, solicitous uncles
offering refuge, protected us until the next tide
of fear eclipsed our progress, sent us into hiding.

Faceless Gabriel Heater rang weekly bombing alerts
into our ears. During 'lights out,' air raid wardens
patrolling the neighborhood were the good men
with families who had been spared from service;

sirens announced the end of war alerts;
in the bowels of buildings, shelters no one ever
entered housed foreign-speaking custodians
we trusted with our lives.

Our 'just cause' war's victorious end
would restore the dream we all believed --
our Home of the Brave, Land of the Free, would prevail.

A son and daughter named for the treasured dead,
we embraced mother's family of modest Ukrainians
whose complex syllabic identity disappeared on Ellis Island.

Their ghosts have found lodging within us;
our house and its foundation were built
from every loss and each survival,

its shines and stains live on in our grown children
attempting to free themselves of the past,
reform mortared bricks into their growing lives.

Roadtrip West

A bright thought flies across my afternoon
fighting to stay aloft as my finger, on an old roadmap

traces a trip across the desert decades ago,
driving west in the early summer of our marriage.

We traveled by night in a compact car,
small dog panting in the backseat.

We fled scalding walls of heat toward
an ocean we could only picture.

Even trailer trucks behind us huffing across
the Rockies could not make us give way,

nor fog banks or detours we met full face;
challenged, we pressed north to the redwoods.

These things I knew: we were young and capable;
this was our America, our luck to belong here.

We were pursuing an instinct to find our edge,
look back at our innocence from a distance.

We saw rooms confining our aspirations,
doors to push open to a maze of choices.

A Bit of Sunlight that Got Caught in Stone

in memory of my brother, Robert S.

The old fathers who bow
down to their sons on their knees
never placed a hand on my brother's shoulder.

He entered shadows without a guide
entered loneliness without blessing.

Only three chairs stood around the table
where he sat dreaming, speculating.
The hands of compassionate women
filled his cup with milk.
The bitter brew of the fathers
almost killed his appetite.

All his youth he had a need for sugar.
All his life a need to understand
how and why to hold a sword.

My Line

The open air platform
at Brighton Beach
elevated two gritty flights
above bustling shops on
the Avenue, was scratchy,
sandy and busy with bodies.
Summer days, with blankets
dragging, bathing suits still wet,
arms and legs smarting
from hours in the sun,
we smelled like the sea.
The ride home was too fast.

Through open train windows,
cool air soothed our shoulders,
my new best friend quiet now
after so much talking, munching,
racing back the waves.

We disembarked onto
Church Avenue steaming
with hotdog and newsstands,
sooty smoke clouds
from lines of blustering busses.

But it was only Saturday and
tomorrow we'd put together
bags of sandwiches, chips
and soda, baby oil and iodine,
another thick towel
(cigarettes hidden within)
ready to grab another day.

Odors of danger and secret sex
from wet sand under the boardwalk
still ripe in our nostrils.

Mother's instructions to
watch out for the older boys,
change out of wet bathing suits
weighed on us like extra pounds.

Polio overshadowed other
adolescent fears and like FDR
you couldn't get chilled,
overtired or breathe open-mouthed
in the crowded subway cars.

Summers later as a college student,
I found my place beside the workforce
pressed onto the local stops,
the train after DeKalb ascending

the Manhattan Bridge to cross
into alluring worlds of fashion,
insurance and finance.

The BMT -- heady road from
my provincial leafy borough to the City
where the future waited within tall buildings
urging me into rush hours of ambition.

Potatoes

In the dream I repeatedly shop
for groceries at the same market.
Its stock is quite limited;
to get to the check out
you must enter by the back door.

This time my mother is with me
asking the clerk for a side of beef
and bushels of potatoes.
She is expecting a crowd of people
both of us know will never arrive.
I go along with this madness
because she is a good cook,
I love french fries and I can
easily let chunks of beef
slip to the floor for the dogs.

Am I trying to keep her busy
or feed some larger illusion
we have entered together?

We believed that men would
save us if we provided nurturance,
that food would never spoil;
there would always be Sunday dinners.

Over and over I revisit this dream
of preparation and disappointment.
She is the cook; I am the helper at her side.
We keep piling up mounds and mounds
of fleshy potatoes because we
do not know we are in a dream.

An Indian Named Place

The slender tall November tree
fills with glossy angled starlings,
frenetic pinwheels pecking at leftover pods.

A large truck passing with a rush
of thunder sends them into
the air as a swirling single fist.

The bare tree carries me
to my childhood household
when mother left for a weekend,
travelling upstate by rail to
an Indian named place I had never seen.

Hallways, rooms swiftly hollowed
in her absence, my pulsing lifeline cut.

Terror, through the winterbound evening
spread an ominous chiaroscuro --
she would never return, a victim swallowed
by a vast northern landscape,
my lost household, an empty heartcage
would not survive, taking me with it.

I stand before the tree now aware
of its reconfigured silhouette, notice
a few dried leaves form starlike shapes.

Act of Faith

My silver car
slides through fog,
the road's arc
known only
by the tires' treads.

Lights float toward me
as spirit eyes
burning out
all borderlines.

I'm held aloft by
silence dimensional
as a deserted
hospital corridor
magnifying
mother's last sighs.

A drop into a trench
might be close
as the moment
the pellucid drip
no longer enters
her veins
and her skin
suddenly smoothed
is fine snow
under
my fingertips.

Descent

Last night the toothless grin
of a young moon
hung over the desert
where old saguaros
raised their arms
against a frost
stripping down spiny flesh
to bony carcasses
only desert wrens
would peck at.

A spell of rogue weather
unbidden as a phonecall
in the night
carrying dire news.

Another plane parallels ours
across white tundras of cloud,
its tail a snake of cordsmoke
dividing the sky.

Returning east we begin
our descent over the tall
inventory of urban glitz

into a flood of neon
luminescence
obliterating a sullied moon.

Our Spangled Earth

Sept. 2001

More cherished now, our spangled earth
yields astonishing beauty,
an urgent pleasure bordering on pain.

Leaves hold on as we do --
tarnished, older, carrying wounds
of our late summer grief.
In pleated skirts, they flame
against a childish blue sky,
a sustained, dazzling light
challenging our sorrow --
clear young faces of the dead,
their severed lives squandered
in the name of one god or another.

Hasn't there been enough destruction
to satisfy the bitter god of ashes?

What now can we offer the angels of mercy?

Walking with Jesus

My friend is telling me morphine
allowed her hand to push
through the veil into another
dimension she cannot name.
Her other arm reached for
the first, testing her whereabouts.

Then she pushed it through again.
It was like the time, she says,
she walked with Jesus
holding his arm, tears flooding
her pillow in the hospital.

"Your Fate is now, you decide"
appears on the tab of a fortune cookie
she cracks open as we chat
in the local Chinese restaurant.

"They deliver" I tell her,
"maybe this is your time."

She purchases a dozen small bottles
of ginseng to enhance her vision,
fiercely clutches the precious entry passes.

Bequest

It arrived whole
wrapped in coarse
butcher paper
in a sticky envelope
crimson spreading fingers
to the torn edges.

I couldn't show it to anyone,
no cemetery would accept
its nameless bulk.

His heart was mine to freeze
or bury in a glade of woods.

How could I preserve
its lush color, the bold bulge
of its chambers,
the way it evoked language
directly into my ears?

Unwrapped
exposed and free
I slip it down
my blouse to lodge
between my breasts.

I will get used
to the leaking stains
tattooing fiery patterns
on my skin
knowing that I harbor
a secret pacemaker.

Every Grieving Poem

spells loss in its own handwriting
each finds its imagery for ghosts
coming near with outstretched arms;
memories open jaws to bite at our backs
or gouge holes in the throat that call up
reminders of what cannot be ours again --
a smell, a posture so distinct,
or somewhat similar, sought after --
but the vocabulary of grief
ends at a blank page

I don' t understand the meaning
of eight years or twenty;
the three small letters of 'ago'
end in the hollow of an empty circle
rolling through time, concave as an echo
configured small as the mouth of an infant
searching in vain for succor

September When She Called

— *for Eliza*

September when she called
from the far edge of the continent
wailing as the towers plummeted,
vision fractured by barriers of flame,
bodies tumbling from smoky heights
sirens screaming for help
leaderless herds of people
scrambling for emergency air
I urged: look away, run, run to the sea,
find a vastness your eyes can fill
with brocades of white birds crossing
to fragrant islands; escape!

A Meager Diet of Horizon

from a phrase by Elizabeth Bishop

The woman contemplating scraps of sustenance
knew how to manage on *a meager diet of horizon;*
the anemic sky offered nothing but boundaries.

Winter would not creep upon her unprepared;
shortening days generated watercolor moonscapes,
a rash of recklessness and high wire stunts of amnesia

until she'd settle into the loneliness of it, circle the floor,
a feral animal sniffing out a resting place, wed to a famine
of dailiness, the lack of surprise behind every door.

Gusts

In the northeast it takes
the first pounding rain and
siren winds to bring down
garnet lemon leaves.

Powerful gusts of trouble
that come late into life,
testing resources and talents.

The indefinite outline
of what's coming spreads its fog
each time we raise our heads
from what we're doing.

What might have been
lies buried beneath leaf piles;
under our thick soled shoes
dry chords splinter
into overtures of change.

Putting Lilli Down

1.
She is walking an edge
between survival and release,
an old woman dragging her bones,
an innocent entering a forest.

How wide is the ribbon of her will --
is it taut or slack as netting?

Her eyes are clouded uncertainty.
Cirrus threads trail across winter skies.

2.
Flesh is silently leaving her frame.
Daily there is less of her
hunched on the soft cushion.

The bones pronounce themselves outward.
She is an inverted cage
any loud noise or wind could crack.

3.
Her eyes are silent when I ask if she wants to leave.
She turns away as I moisten her lips.
The coming decision meets me at every turn.

4.
I wish her into sweet sleep.
Let soft fog protect her from pain,
this gentle one who trusted the world.

5.
When we are both ready the day will be very long.
Many years... How do I no longer care for her life?

6.
I carry her to the car,
one hand flat across her back
grateful she does not make a sound.

At the vet's office she settles her body
humbly on the steel table
covered in dark green cloth.

7.
She moves down easily into slumber.
My hands feel no difference
when the second injection stills her heart.

8.
Her drift into death is seamless.
Her open eyes are clear dark glass.

November Ladybugs

A crippled little troupe,
they huddle in the metal
of each other's wings.
Houses on fire, children crisped.

Neutered from drought,
a burned-out summer,
they have surrendered
their faith in family.

Thumbtacks at the seam
of ceilings and walls,
they line up to fasten
my broken house.

Then brown as tooth sockets
after blunt extractions,
the scabs drop, rattle
into pots, pile dry as lentils.

Rat-a-tat-tat
Pox on pans already soiled,
a steady hail of used buckshot
when the hunt's long over.

Shelter Dog

Now I can bury the guilt
I carried abandoning
my companion who
walked beside me
through walls of tall trees
by the old cemetery,
tread the rickety
footbridge to freedom
we crossed together.

I've learned she lived out
her life with an aged couple
on a green hillside
cared for to the end.

When she runs now
into my dreams,
her golden body
finds a soft place,
silky paws stretched out
in parallel comfort.

Call It Romance

At the intersection,
one fork curves left,
the other is straight
as an honest ruler.

I follow the looping curve
to a hillside hamlet.
White clapboard houses perch
on either side, sunshine
glinting in storybook calm,
windows facing a blue river.

In a small park at a picnic table
beneath the shade of a large elm,
an old man and woman
in a floppy hat bend toward one another.

They are still in the thrill of it.
The man goes to the car
to bring her a sweater and
drapes it around her shoulders.

She looks up at him as if
songbirds from the protective tree
were serenading her grace.

I hurtle my car into reverse.

The straightforward road
brings me to a country store
where I seek consolation
in a paper bag of sweets,
a loaf of warm bread.

Departure

An eagerness to open
as the moon widens is the answer
her body offers
before the question is asked.

Desire quivers his breath
as her lips begin to part but
his hesitation stumbles into
a long pause breaking the current.

Lights click off that won't
turn down the covers,
smooth the bedsheets
or honor her hips.

He has slipped out
of the embrace and backs out
of the connection toward
the downhill driveway.

Her orphaned body hardens
into an armored posture
plated by what remains
of her dignity.

Doors and windows
clamp shut for the season.

Daylight peeks in at her still
reviewing the smoldering look
his eyes could not sustain,
the moves his body refused.

Skeins of Yarn

A ball of yarn unravels at my feet --
versions of our years together
exposed in loops and tangles,
knots I pick at after hours,
facets of myself freed up
through stages
of expansion and diminishment.

The cat whomping it across
the floor reveals in her mastery
and delight the complex nature
of intertwining strands.

When the yardage
stretched taut cannot bridge
the space between one human
and another, one gender
and the other, it snaps.

Then each end, frayed and
rootless wanders the floorboards
of the knitting shoppe
for new colors, textures --
a mix like alpaca and
mohair that might cohere
into resilient cloth.

Old Town Home, Albuquerque

1.
Wherever I am I long for home;
smooth weight-bearing arms of adobe
suggest an embrace;
the azure pan above sizzles with color.

Home at the end of a lifelong search;
my body wants to claim its square of earth
the way the centuries old church rests in global sun.

How silence outlasts noise and din,
finds the organic resonance of *home/now/one.*

2.
We were feeling we had seen it all --
cities, mountains, faces, our brains over-wrinkled,
when the sinking sun, turning the air violet
lit the mountains behind a shade of peppery pink -
Sandia, the watermelon hills.

3.
Robert* says be proud we have 'kept our small boats afloat.'
Sorrow, heavy at my core, rolls its Anasazi flutesong,
dark woodwinds breath through canyons of longing.

4.
I will miss my children
miss seeing who they become
when they are my age.

5.
Grief leaves a painful sharpness to attack the body
but sorrow blows the sandstone wind deeper red;
double o's form in the throat the shape of woe
and a penetrating comfort of familiarity.

*poet Robert Bly from *My Sentence Was a Thousand Years of Joy*

Sleeping in Snow

— *for Leo*

"So far so good. The brilliant days and
nights are breathless in their hurry.
We follow, you and I."

— Linda Pastan from "Curriculum Vitae"

Two figures
sleeping in snow
curve into an infinity sign

One of the pair,
I am no longer
decreasing my self

White galaxy dust
of the comet's tail
patinas our form

For this time, this place
we endure, frozen sculpture
in the falling snow

ABOUT THE AUTHOR:

Natalie Safir's long career in poetry includes editing, lecturing, publishing poems in numerous literary journals, running a long-term reading series, teaching private as well as public writing workshops in local institutions, and authoring five collections of poems. Her poem "Matisse's Dance" has been anthologized in college texts by The McGraw Hill Co. and in *Art & Artists*, Everyman edition, Knopf, 2012. Her Jungian fairytale, "The Woman with Midnight Hair" was published in 2010. She taught memoir workshops at a local senior center and currently runs "Stories I Tell My Friends" at the Warner Library in Tarrytown.

Residing in Tarrytown, NY, she is a certified empowerment coach practicing Dreamwork.

Books by Dos Madres Press

Mary Margaret Alvarado - *Hey Folly* (2013)

John Anson - *Jose-Maria de Heredia's Les Trophées* (2013),
   Time Pieces - poems & translations (2014),

Jennifer Arin - *Ways We Hold* (2012)

Michael Autrey - *From The Genre Of Silence* (2008)

Stuart Bartow - *Einstein's Lawn* (2015)

Paul Bray - *Things Past and Things to Come* (2006), *Terrible Woods* (2008)

Ann Cefola - *Face Painting in the Dark* (2014)

Eduardo Chirinos - *Still Life with Flies [naturaleza muerta con moscas]*
   (2016), Bilingual, translated by Gregory Racz

Jon Curley - *New Shadows* (2009), *Angles of Incidents* (2012)

Grace Curtis - *The Shape of a Box* (2014)

Kevin Cutrer - *Lord's Own Anointed* (2015)

Sara Dailey - *Earlier Lives* (2012)

Dennis Daly - *Nightwalking with Nathaniel-poems of Salem* (2014)

Richard Darabaner - *Plaint* (2012)

Deborah Diemont - *Wanderer* (2009), *Diverting Angels* (2012)

Joseph Donahue - *The Copper Scroll* (2007)

Annie Finch - *Home Birth* (2004)

Norman Finkelstein - *An Assembly* (2004), *Scribe* (2009),
   The Ratio of Reason to Magic: New & Selected Poems (2015)

Karen George - *Swim Your Way Back* (2014)

Gerry Grubbs - *Still Life* (2005), *Girls in Bright Dresses Dancing* (2010),
   The Hive-a book we read for its honey (2013)

Richard Hague - *Burst, Poems Quickly* (2004),
   During The Recent Extinctions (2012), *Where Drunk Men Go* (2015)

Ruth D. Handel - *Tugboat Warrior* (2013), *No Border is Perennial* (2015)

Pauletta Hansel - *First Person* (2007), *What I Did There* (2011),
   Tangle (2015)

Michael Heller - *A Look at the Door with the Hinges Off* (2006),
   Earth and Cave (2006)

Michael Henson - *The Tao of Longing & The Body Geographic* (2010)

R. Nemo Hill - *When Men Bow Down* (2012), *In No Man's Ear* (2016)

W. Nick Hill - *And We'd Understand Crows Laughing* (2012), *Blue Nocturne* (2016)

Eric Hoffman - *Life At Braintree* (2008), *The American Eye* (2011), *By the Hours* (2013), *Forms of Life* (2015)

Roald Hoffmann - *Something That Belongs To You* (2015)

James Hogan - *Rue St. Jacques* (2005)

Keith Holyoak - *My Minotaur* (2010), *Foreigner* (2012), *The Gospel According to Judas* (2015)

Nancy Kassell - *Text(isles)* (2013)

David M. Katz - *Claims of Home* (2011), *Stanzas on Oz* (2015)

Sherry Kearns - *Deep Kiss* (2013), *The Magnificence of Ruin* (2015)

Marjorie Deiter Keyishian - *Ashes and All* (2015)

Burt Kimmelman - *There Are Words* (2007), *The Way We Live* (2011)

Jill Kelly Koren - *The Work of the Body* (2015)

Ralph La Charity - *Farewellia a la Aralee* (2014)

Pamela L. Laskin - *Plagiarist* (2012)

Owen Lewis - *Sometimes Full of Daylight* (2013), *Best Man* (2015)

Richard Luftig - *Off The Map* (2006)

Austin MacRae - *The Organ Builder* (2012)

Mario Markus - *Chemical Poems-One For Each Element* (2013)

J. Morris - *The Musician, Approaching Sleep* (2006)

Patricia Monaghan - *Mary-A Life in Verse* (2014)

Rick Mullin - *Soutine* (2012), *Coelacanth* (2013), *Sonnets on the Voyage of the Beagle* (2014), *Stignatz & the User of Vicenza* (2015)

Fred Muratori - *A Civilization* (2014)

Robert Murphy - *Not For You Alone* (2004), *Life in the Ordovician* (2007), *From Behind The Blind* (2013)

Pam O'Brien - *The Answer To Each Is The Same* (2012)

Peter O'Leary - *A Mystical Theology of the Limbic Fissure* (2005)

Sharon Olinka - *Old Ballerina Club* (2016)

Bea Opengart - *In The Land* (2011)

David A. Petreman - *Candlelight in Quintero-bilingual ed.* (2011)

Paul Pines - *Reflections in a Smoking Mirror* (2011),
    New Orleans Variations & Paris Ouroboros (2013),
    Fishing on the Pole Star (2014)
    Message from the Memoirist (2015)

Quanita Roberson - *Soul Growing-Wisdom for thirteen year old boys
    from men around the world* (2015)

William Schickel - *What A Woman* (2007)

Don Schofield - *In Lands Imagination Favors* (2014)

David Schloss - *Behind the Eyes* (2005),
    Reports from Babylon and Beyond (2015)

Daniel Shapiro - *The Red Handkerchief and other poems* (2014)

Murray Shugars - *Songs My Mother Never Taught Me* (2011),
    Snakebit Kudzu (2013)

Jason Shulman - *What does reward bring you but to bind you to
    Heaven like a slave? (2013)*

Maxine Silverman - *Palimpsest (2014)*

Lianne Spidel & Anne Loveland - *Pairings* (2012),
    A Bird in the Hand (2014)

Olivia Stiffler - *Otherwise, we are safe* (2013)

Carole Stone - *Hurt, the Shadow-the Josephine Hopper poems* (2013)

Nathan Swartzendruber - *Opaque Projectionist* (2009)

Jean Syed - *Sonnets* (2009)

Eileen R. Tabios - *INVENT[ST]ORY Selected Catalog Poems and New
    1996-2015* (2015)

Madeline Tiger - *The Atheist's Prayer* (2010), *From the Viewing Stand* (2011)

James Tolan - *Red Walls* (2011)

Brian Volck - *Flesh Becomes Word* (2013)

Henry Weinfield - *The Tears of the Muses* (2005),
    Without Mythologies (2008), *A Wandering Aramaean* (2012)

Donald Wellman - *A North Atlantic Wall* (2010),
    The Cranberry Island Series (2012)
Sarah White - *The Unknowing Muse* (2014)
Anne Whitehouse - *The Refrain* (2012)
Martin Willetts Jr. - *Secrets No One Must Talk About* (2011)
Tyrone Williams - *Futures, Elections* (2004), *Adventures of Pi* (2011)
Geoffrey Woolf - *Learn to Love Explosives* (2016)
David Almaleck Wolinsky - *The Crane is Flying - Early Poems* (2016)
Kip Zegers - *The Poet of Schools* (2013), *The Pond in Room 318* (2015)

www.dosmadres.com